REDEEMING HALLOWEEN

REDEEMING HALLOWEEN

Clay Bridges
PRESS

MATT SARGEANT

Redeeming Halloween
Copyright © 2023 by Matt Sargeant

Published by Lucid Books in Houston, TX
www.LucidBooks.com

All rights reserved. No part of this publication may be reproduced, stored in a retrieval system, or transmitted in any form by any means, electronic, mechanical, photocopy, recording, or otherwise, without the prior permission of the publisher, except as provided for by USA copyright law.

Unless otherwise indicated, scripture quotations are taken from the ESV® Bible (The Holy Bible, English Standard Version®), copyright © 2001 by Crossway, a publishing ministry of Good News Publishers. Used by permission. All rights reserved.

eISBN: 978-1-68488-067-6
ISBN: 978-1-68488-066-9 Paperback

Special Sales: Lucid Books titles are available in special quantity discounts. Custom imprinting or excerpting can also be done to fit special needs. Contact Lucid Books at Info@LucidBooks.com

Dedication

To Lisa,
My wife, best friend, and biggest supporter.
I will never see myself the way you do,
but you make me believe I can be more than what I see.

Table of Contents

Prologue 1

Part I: History of Halloween 3
    Chapter 1: Pagan Superstition 5
    Chapter 2: Religious Observance 11
    Chapter 3: Western Consumerism 19

Part II: Truths of Scripture 23
    Chapter 4: Redemption of Culture 25
    Chapter 5: Celebration of Death 35
    Chapter 6: Return of Christ 47

Part III: Cause for Celebration 67
    Chapter 7: Reasons to Celebrate 69
    Chapter 8: Ways to Celebrate 77

Epilogue 93

Prologue

The moment I feel that first crisp air in early September, there is something in my soul that ignites. Throughout my adult life, fall has been my favorite season by far. While I do appreciate each season for what it is, fall wins in a head-to-head competition with any other season, hands down. There is no better weather than an ideal autumn day. The colors of nature during that time of year are unrivaled. The sights, the smells, the tastes – all of it thrills a part of me deep inside in a way I cannot adequately explain. That excitement is why my family typically starts decorating our house with fake fall leaves, scarecrows, and orange lights weeks before the autumnal equinox. If you live in a part of the world where fall does not arrive in all of its sensational glory like it does where I live in western New York, then I am sad that you have been cheated of one of life's purest pleasures.

As fall arrives and progresses, added to the harvest décor are ghosts, jack-o'-lanterns, bats, and a host of other eerie creatures.

After I began to trust the Lord when I was in junior high, Halloween gave me mixed emotions up until my 30s. While part of me remained fascinated by all things spooky, many elements of our culture's Halloween appeared to counter a life of faith in God, and so my fascination was suppressed by guilt.

It was not my own conviction that brought me to this guilt-ridden conclusion, however. The church overwhelmingly ignores and often opposes any connection to Halloween. As a Christian myself, I felt obligated to follow in step.

It is easy to see why many conservative followers of Jesus struggle with acknowledging Halloween and often run from, ignore, or even combat it. For better or worse, these people often raise an eyebrow at any believer who is not in agreement with the seeming consensus. However, in this book, I want to argue that it is my faith in Jesus that inspires me to participate in the festivities that come at the end of October.

There is spiritual significance to Halloween that rivals that of the two big Christian holidays, but October 31 often gets neutered or thrown out by well-meaning believers. I strongly believe there is a unique opportunity here for Christians which is largely being missed because either we celebrate Halloween as a holiday with no spiritual significance or we ignore (and even condemn) Halloween altogether. Both the history behind the holiday, as well as the spiritual truths laid out in the Bible, give believers every reason to take yet another thing the world has corrupted and redeem it for eternal use in our families, churches, and communities.

PART I
HISTORY
OF
HALLOWEEN

CHAPTER ONE

Pagan Superstition

Any attempt to appropriately enjoy Halloween is greatly aided by a knowledge of its history. Explaining the meaning behind the celebration itself as well as the practices that have led to our modern-day traditions will bring to light what may and may not be proper for a sincere believer in Jesus to practice. Having been enlightened by the Holy Spirit's ministry as we study the Scriptures, Christians can survey the history of Halloween and come confidently to conclusions regarding how their families can tastefully observe this celebration.

While the direct causes of most of the traditions associated with Halloween are unclear, the holiday we know today is the product of three primary root influences: pagan superstition, religious observance, and Western consumerism. We begin with pagan superstition because, in it, Halloween likely has its earliest origin.

Some people will argue that Halloween had its initial beginning in the church, but it is at least as likely that the church's roots in a mid-fall festival were a reaction to pagan practices of that time. It is Halloween's heathen origin that has caused, whether directly or indirectly, many well-meaning Christians to be wary of our culture's October 31 celebrations. I suggest no such concern is necessary, as the two most significant dates on the Christian calendar, Easter and Christmas, also have early roots in paganism, making them no different from Halloween.

SAMHAIN

Halloween appears to have its earliest inspiration somewhere around the time of Christ in the geographic area that today is made up of Ireland, the United Kingdom, and northern France. This land was inhabited by the ancient Celtics during that time.

Between the autumnal equinox and the winter solstice, the Celtics would begin their new year with a three-day festival called Samhain (pronounced "saa-wn.") To this day, Samhain is still observed by the Irish people. The name means "summer's end," and the festivities begin on October 31 and end on November 2.

We notice that as fall progresses, the days get colder and the nights come earlier. Winter is right around the corner, and with it, nature brings darkness, cold, and death. For the Celtics, Samhain was a time to complete their harvest activities in preparation for the dark winter and also to come together and pray to their false gods, while offering animal sacrifices.

A major activity in this celebration was lighting a large bonfire, from which sacred source the people would take fire back to their homes to light their personal hearths. The light from these large fires would, naturally, attract a lot of insects, which in turn brought bats – and so the winged mammals became associated with this season and, like the season, with death.

Perhaps the most significant belief regarding Samhain as it influences our modern celebration of Halloween is the myth that the veil between our physical world and the spiritual world is at its thinnest – or even lifted altogether – during these three days of the year. With this barrier no longer an obstacle, spirits who had departed earth would be able to temporarily return to the physical world.

This myth was one of hope for some, as many people welcomed the return of a deceased loved one, often leaving food out or even a seat at the meal table for him or her. For others, this belief inspired terror, especially if a person was guilty of having wronged someone who, now departed, may return with vengeful intentions. In addition, this thinning or lifting of the veil may have been believed to pave the way for not only spirits of the human dead, but also more malevolent beings, such as ghouls and demons.

In order to protect himself or herself from evil spirits during Samhain, one would wear a disguise or costume. Should the disguised individual encounter a friendly spirit, the wearer could remove his or her mask to be recognized by the beloved departed friend. Otherwise, the costume would, as it was believed, allow the wearer to remain undetected by evil spirits, who would mistake the living person for another denizen of the spiritual world that had crossed over. These costumes may have even been used to scare away ghosts and demons, and thus protect one's family and property.

In addition, it is suspected that food was left out, not only as a gift for a welcomed spirit but as an appeasement for those less pleasant ghosts. It stands to reason that a vengeful spirit that came across a gift would be less likely to execute its malicious intentions. This treat was believed to deter a wicked spirit from bringing upon the household a disastrous trick.

Another Samhain practice that began centuries later was the carving and lighting of turnips designed to keep spirits away. These makeshift lamps were and still are referred to today as jack-o'-lanterns, so named after the Legend of Stingy Jack.

Whether Jack was the name of an actual person or just a placeholder name for a generic character is uncertain. Either way, this Jack was an unpleasant character who was said to have tricked the devil on multiple occasions. One such instance was when Jack refused to pay for the devil's drink (hence, "Stingy" Jack), and another time when Jack trapped the devil in a tree by carving a cross into the bark.

As the legend goes, the end result of Jack's tricks was that Satan bargained to never claim Jack's soul after death. When Jack did die, his sinful life disqualified him from heaven. However, the devil honored his agreement to not claim Jack's soul but threw burning coal from hell at Jack. (We understand from Scripture that Satan does not actually permit or deny access to hell, nor does he reside there, but bear with me for the sake of this story). To help stave off the cold and darkness, Jack carved out a turnip in which to place the coal, giving him a light for his way as he remained eternally cursed to wander the darkness of the earth.

From this legend, when people would see an unexplained light in the darkness, they would say it was "Jack of the lantern," which contracted to "Jack-o'-lantern." During the 19th century, people began to make their own jack-o'-lanterns, carving faces into turnips to scare off Jack or other spirits like him. These jack-o'-lanterns may have been placed on a window ledge or outside the home as a charm for protection and even carried about for those same reasons as people went outside – likely disguised, as was the case during Samhain – during this eerie time of year when supernatural activity was believed to be at its height.

As centuries progressed and people began to better understand the world around them, fear of spirits turned into a fascination with the supernatural. Children began to dress up as ghosts for fun rather than disguise themselves to hide from ghosts. With this interest, so began the tradition of pulling pranks intended to make the trick appear to have been performed by a supernatural being. Thus began a long-standing tradition of pranks among the people of the Celtic region.

POMONA

At one point, most of the Celtic territory was occupied by the Roman Empire. As Roman culture permeated this region, so also did Roman festivals. Rome already had its own celebration of the dead called Feralia, which took place in February. Feralia did not have an apparent affect on Samhain, probably because the holidays were months apart.

A fall holiday the Romans may have celebrated was Pomona, which honored the goddess of fruit bearing the same name. Pomona is believed to have taken place in early November, possibly coinciding with the Samhain festival of the Celtics which had been conquered. It is possible this celebration influenced autumn festivities in the Celtic region. Pomona's association with apples has likely given way to some fall traditions often associated with Halloween, including apple picking, drinking apple cider, and bobbing for apples.

While modern Halloween themes are predominantly dark and spooky, this was not always so for celebrations during this time of year. Perhaps thanks to the influence of Pomona, there was a strong emphasis on romance as a component of these mid-fall festivities during the Middle Ages. The first person to successfully catch an apple in bobbing for apples was said to be the next one to marry. As another example of this type of superstitious tradition, a woman would peel an apple and throw the skin behind her back, expecting the peel to fall in the form of the first initial of the man she was to marry.

CONCLUSION

Much like the holiday itself, the pagan origins of Halloween are shrouded in mystery and myth. Not much is known for certain about the ancient fall celebrations and their role in the evolution of the holiday now observed every year at the end of October. From what we do know, however, it is easy to see some of the connections between these pagan practices from thousands of years ago and some of the traditions we carry out today.

CHAPTER TWO

Religious Observance

While the specific impact of paganism on our subject is unclear in many regards, more is known with certainty regarding the influences of religion on modern Halloween, particularly from the Catholic church. Now, while some Christians may be uncomfortable with Halloween's pagan influences, Protestants within Christendom may be just as wary of Halloween's Catholic roots. As a Reformed Christian myself, I am aware of many of the Catholic church's misguided teachings; however, just as the pagan inspirations behind Halloween do not disqualify Protestants from participating in these mid-fall festivities, neither does its association with the Catholic church.

ALLHALLOWSTIDE
Origin

While I suspect your calendar does not mark the observance of Samhain, there is a good chance that it denotes November 1 as

All Saints Day. In the fifth century, Pope Boniface IV instituted All Saints as a feast day when he dedicated the Pantheon in Rome to Mary. It became a time to honor those heroes of the faith who had departed to be with the Lord. It is important to note here that heroes of the faith refer to those special individuals whom the Catholic church denotes as "saints"; however, the Bible refers to saints as anyone who has put his or her faith in Jesus.

All Saints Day was initially held on May 13. In the eighth century, Pope Gregory III moved the date to November 1 when he dedicated the Vatican chapel in honor of all saints collectively. It was then Pope Gregory IV who instituted November 2 as All Souls Day, a day to honor not just Catholic saints, but all departed souls who had been redeemed. Remember that November 2 was the third and final day of the Samhain festival as well.

All Saints, as with many feast days in the European Medieval church, was preceded by an evening of prayer and fasting. In this case, that night, October 31, was called All Hallows Eve (meaning All Saints Evening, celebrated similarly to how we celebrate Christmas Eve in our culture.) This three-day period from October 31 to November 2 became known as "Allhallowstide" and was a time to remember the dead, particularly saints and martyrs, but also all faithful departed Christians.

Traditions

A significant focus of the Catholic celebration of Allhallowstide from its inception was praying for the dead. The Catholic church believes in purgatory, a place where the souls of the dead arrive after life ends to complete payment for their lesser sins before being accepted into heaven. Of course, the Bible teaches that those who have put their faith in Christ's atoning work on the cross have no need for additional payment and are, therefore, welcomed into heaven immediately upon death. Conversely, the wicked arrive immediately in hell, as salvation is not of works (Ephesians 2) and, therefore, no amount of payment for their sins could earn them a place in heaven one day.

However, with this false belief of purgatory prevailing, impoverished people in Europe during the 15th century began to go door-to-door in wealthier neighborhoods, offering prayers for that family's departed loved ones to receive food. The food prepared was often pastries that came to be known as "soul cakes," which were given in exchange for prayers for the souls of the dead supposedly in purgatory. Hence, the practice became known as "souling" and would go on to be practiced primarily by children.

About a century later, "mumming" or "guising" became popular in Ireland and the surrounding areas. Like souling, guising involved people going to neighborhood houses asking for food, only these guisers were so-called because they, like their Celtic ancestors, were disguised in costumes. Instead of offering prayers for the dead, the guisers typically sang or otherwise entertained the homeowners in hope of receiving gifts.

Connection

Allhallowstide has been branded as its own set of holy days, separate from Samhain, but the similarities between the two are obvious. For example, some Catholics began to believe that after someone died, his or her soul wandered the earth until All Saints Day. This meant that All Hallows Eve was the spirit's last chance to take care of unfinished business. It was a particularly frightful notion if this spirit was vengeful.

Other spooky beliefs began to permeate religious minds during this time of year throughout the Middle Ages as well, such as a fear of black cats that were suspected to be companions to witches or actually shape-shifting witches themselves. The Samhain belief that the presence of a bat preceded death also persisted throughout Medieval times.

While some people, particularly in the Catholic church, see the overlap of Allhallowstide and Samhain as coincidental, it can be easily argued that the strong connection between the two was determined by more than simple chance. Even though some people believe that Pope Gregory III was not aware of Samhain, the fact that the Christian feast honoring the dead was moved to the middle of a similar pagan festival strongly suggests that someone in the church was aware of the connection. Include the All Hallows Eve vigil and the third Allhallowstide day of All Souls, and the connection between the sets of three-day festivities is almost undeniable.

In fact, the Catholic church has a history of redeeming pagan practices to facilitate evangelism. Cultural practices, after all, often mean more to the individuals in that society than simply the meaning behind a given observance. These practices become part of one's identity. At the same time, some of these activities may be inconsistent with the teachings of the Bible, or, as may have been the case in these situations, the teaching of the church at the time.

In the Middle Ages, as the Catholic church's teaching spread abroad and encountered new cultures, incorporating pagan festivities into church observances promised a smoother transition for new converts than imploring them to abandon all of their pagan practices, many of which were certainly ingrained within their lives. These church observances offered an alternative to pagan activities for new Christians, allowing, in some sense, for the converts not to separate from harmless family traditions that had become part of who they were. A textbook example of this type of cultural incorporation is Christmas Day, as the church placed its celebration of the nativity to intentionally overlap with the cultural winter festival that had become characterized by drinking and revelry.

GUY FAWKES DAY

Another stop on our timeline of the religious influence on modern Halloween came on November 5, 1605, with the establishment of Guy Fawkes Day. Following the Gunpowder Plot, a Catholic group's failed attempt to assassinate the protestant King James I of Britain, Guy Fawkes was captured. Fawkes's role in the plot is often debated, but since he was caught, his name is attached to the memory of the event.

British Protestants began to celebrate Guy Fawkes Day on November 5 as a win for Protestants. The celebration became characterized by vandalistic events targeting Catholic establishments. Even children would go out on this day, visiting houses and threatening vandalism if they were not placated with a treat.

AMERICAN HALLOWEEN

As time went on, the name All Hallows Eve became Hallows Eve, which became Hallow e'en, and finally, the name we know it by today, Halloween. By this time, Halloween had made its way to America, but primarily only in regions like Maryland and southward where the Catholic presence was much more prominent.

Up north, the people were largely Protestant, many of whom were Puritans who took a very separatist approach to worldly and Catholic practices. Halloween did not fit into their paradigm. The Puritans did, however, continue to recognize Guy Fawkes Day as their victory over Catholicism. This celebration eventually died out around the time of the American Revolution. The only component of Guy Fawkes Day to remain was vandalism.

Halloween remained a regional celebration in the United States until the 19th century when more Europeans immigrated to North America, bringing with them their own traditions and celebrations. The event that likely caused the most pronounced impact on Halloween in America was the Irish Potato Famine, which convinced many people to flee from Ireland to the United States.

With them, the Irish brought their tradition of carving jack-o'-lanterns. However, with pumpkins more plentiful in America than they were in Ireland and easier to carve than turnips, it was at this time that pumpkins began to be used for jack-o'-lanterns. Jack-o'-lanterns would be carried by children when they went souling or guising as a source of light and as protection from wicked spirits.

The Irish, continuing on the tradition that had its inception with Samhain, particularly enjoyed playing pranks at Halloween.

Coupled with the propensity to vandalize from Guy Fawkes Day, pranking incidents increased and became more and more dangerous, especially as Halloween celebrations moved from rural communities to the cities.

What started as simple fun went entirely too far, making Halloween the height of mischievous behavior on the American calendar. During the Great Depression, vandalism and violence reached their peak, causing great concern over the celebration of Halloween. There was even talk of banning the holiday altogether.

To combat this danger, people began to organize activities like Halloween parties and haunted houses to keep kids off the street. These events gave children a fun alternative to destructive behavior, capitalizing on the spookiness associated with the season. It was also reported that some people began giving out small tokens to potential vandals, who agreed to leave the homeowners in peace in exchange for a treat. While the exact origin of the phrase "trick-or-treat" is lost, what we today refer to as trick-or-treating had its genesis under these circumstances.

CONTINUED OBSERVANCE

At this point, you may be wondering if we are even still talking about religious observance anymore. Interestingly, we can trace haunted houses, vandalism, and trick-or-treating back to spiritual inspiration one way or another, even if these traditions are stripped of most if not all of their religious motivation. That said, there are still faith-based observances held on Halloween around the world today, though its secular observance is far more predominant in

North America. Regardless, some Catholic groups will hold services this year on Halloween and light candles for the dead, whether at home, at a church, or in a cemetery. Halloween is still observed as a day to pray for souls that are in purgatory in hopes of aiding these souls toward heaven.

Among Protestants, Halloween became and continues to be an opportunity for remembering the Reformation. After all, it was on October 31, 1517, that Martin Luther famously posted his 95 Theses to combat the false teachings of the Catholic church. It is believed that Luther picked All Hallows Eve on purpose because of the prevailing teaching of praying for the dead, one of many Catholic doctrines that Luther aimed to expose as inconsistent with the Bible. Thus, the Protestant Reformation officially began, and so the day continues to be celebrated annually by many Protestants. Some Protestants today, in honor of what has become known as Reformation Day, hold Reformation parties where guests dress as different reformers or heroes of the faith (rather than ghosts and monsters) and hand out gospel tracts along with candy to trick-or-treaters.

It has been a long, winding road that has brought us from a Celtic festival millennia ago, through church observances, and finally, to the Halloween we know today. What we practice today in October is directly linked to the religious roots of the holiday, while maintaining undeniable influence from prior pagan festivities. However, man's spiritual fascination does not account for all of what we are familiar with regarding our own Halloween celebrations. There is one more root influencing today's holiday that did not come about until after World War II.

CHAPTER THREE

Western Consumerism

Just about any Halloween tradition can be traced back to a pagan myth or a religious belief. Understandably, given the background and evolution of the holiday, there was and remains some discomfort surrounding Halloween, especially with people who consider themselves to be more conservative. If you are in that camp, the third influence should not make you feel any better. While the true meaning behind Halloween and its traditions are rooted in myth and faith, there is primarily one thing that has turned Halloween into the significant date on the calendar we know today: money.

It is unlikely Halloween would be as big as it is in our times without the aid of consumerism. While each practice we have mentioned up until now can be traced back to holidays like Samhain or All Saints Day, none of the historical celebrations account for the amount of horror and product placement that are commonplace with Halloween now. There was an entirely different motivation behind those aspects of our mid-fall festivities.

Remember, before Halloween reached the popularity it has today, some people were calling for the abolition of Halloween due to the ramping up of dangerous activity. It is not far-fetched to think that without consumerism, Halloween would perhaps be limited to some isolated celebrations around the country. In fact, at this point, I cannot really imagine Halloween without marketing. Sooner or later, a business was going to see those trick-or-treaters dressed up in ghost costumes and realize the money-making potential there. Once the energy behind the violence was channeled into parties and attractions, eventually capitalistic America was going to see an opportunity to, well, capitalize.

PRODUCT PLACEMENT

With the rise of haunted houses, costume contests, parties, and trick-or-treating came a decline in vandalism and violence. What also came was an increase in demand for supplies for these festivities. It did not take long for companies to step up and meet that demand.

Have you ever wondered what superheroes, princesses, and television characters have to do with the origins of Halloween? Nothing! There is no connection between Elsa and the Celtics. Baby Shark has literally nothing to do with honoring the dead. Spiderman did not cross over to the physical world during Samhain. The reason you can buy a costume of just about anything these days is that businesses wanted to market their product or draw attention to the business with a popular program, particularly in the 1950s when affordable costumes began to be produced. It was around the same time that sugar rationing ceased following World War II, causing candy production and sales to pick up.

CANDY

Candy is another significant part of modern Halloween with no spiritually meaningful historical root. The treats given out to trick-or-treaters were originally things like nuts, fruit, coins, and toys. Candy was not predominantly associated with Halloween until the companies that manufactured and sold candy seized the opportunity. Today, while the threat of vandalism does not loom as large as it did in the past, I would advise against handing out nuts to trick-or-treaters!

For the next few decades after World War II, kids would find a good mix of treats in their goodie bags on Halloween night. By the close of the 1970s, parents felt safer having their children receive sealed, store-bought candy as opposed to loose, random items from a stranger's home. The candy companies had done their work, and now candy is essentially the exclusive treat of Halloween.

ENTERTAINMENT

Retail products cannot take all the credit for making Halloween the commercial success it is today. Hollywood is another money-making industry that has directed the course of Halloween since the 20th century. Horror movies are going to exist whether Halloween is popular or not, but there is no better time for the makers of horror films to capitalize on a movie release than the season when people have historically been more likely to ponder death and spooky things.

Today, homes across North America tune into scary movies all throughout October. Some television stations air these types of movies almost exclusively. Streaming apps provide centralized hubs of Halloween-appropriate viewing, making it even easier for consumers to get into the Halloween spirit.

As Hollywood has done with many other aspects of our culture, it intensified the scary aspects of Halloween to shock and entertain audiences to boost movie sales. Intending to increase the horror to make films more interesting, not only did movie monsters get scarier, gore and violence were introduced as themes of Halloween.

As these graphic images took over the big screen, they made their way into costumes and decorations too. It is the same mindset that has inspired other forms of entertainment, including elaborate haunted houses and Halloween parties all across the continent, to go down the same sensationalized path. Someone behind each event is hoping to make a buck, and more intense scares promise more sales.

Owners of retail products and event production companies have influenced Halloween to make it as mainstream and as scary as it is today. The result is billions of dollars spent across the United States on this holiday. Thanks to American consumerism, Halloween is now second only to Christmas as the largest commercial holiday in North America.

PART II
TRUTHS
— OF —
SCRIPTURE

CHAPTER FOUR

Redemption of Culture

The years we covered in our survey of Halloween's history have produced a very unique holiday that many of us celebrate every year on October 31. Up to this point, my aim has been to lay out a factual and objective account of this history. I have limited my personal commentary thus far, unless there was a minor aspect I did not intend to come back to that required the lens of Scripture to clarify.

In the second major section of this book, I intend to take the history and practices associated with Halloween and see how they measure up to God's Word. Regardless of the conclusions we reach, my prayer is that "each one . . . be fully convinced in his own mind" (Romans 14) based on the teachings of the Bible. From there, we can determine personal practices accordingly.

Throughout its history, Halloween has boasted very little true Scriptural value. Even the significant influence of the Catholic church is founded largely on incorrect teaching and borderline idolatry. For example, purgatory does not exist, and the practice of exalting saints above other mortal humans is, in my opinion, forbidden in Scripture, as this exaltation rides awfully close to the worship of man. These revelations delegitimize many of the practices of Allhallowstide from a biblical perspective.

Then there is the pagan genesis of Halloween, born from a festival founded on myth, superstition, and fear – to say nothing about its worship of false deities. The spiritual elements of Samhain are inconsistent with the truths of the Bible, and a believer certainly could not embrace the meaning of this particular holiday in good conscience. We do not need to be motivated by fear and superstition. We can be certain of the spiritual realities around us as far as they affect our daily lives.

While consumerism surely has added some fun to Halloween, it has also overtaken some of the holiday's originally harmless elements and even added new elements, in many cases bringing these facets of the celebration past the point of being tolerable for Christians. Plus, the driving force behind Halloween's explosion in the commercial market is the love of money, which brings about only evil (1 Timothy 6). To be caught up in this mindset would seem to me a lot like being "conformed to the pattern of this world" (Romans 12).

QUESTION OF REDEEMING CULTURE

Do these questionable elements mean Halloween cannot be redeemed? I respect the believer who has done his or her homework on this holiday and concludes that there are too many red flags to allow one's family to participate in Halloween festivities. Remember, Romans 14 teaches us that we can do the right thing and still be guilty of sin if we are violating our conscience. In fact, I would suggest that you should not celebrate Halloween until you have taken the time to think through its origins, meanings, and redemptive qualities.

However, there is much to be said about the validity of observing Halloween. There is rich spiritual truth and a real cause for celebration when we take the elements of this holiday that are not contrary to Scripture and study what God's Word says about these topics. While not everything in our world is inherently spiritual, we can still mine things for biblical truths for our benefit and the benefit of our loved ones. I am talking about books, movies, and, yes, holidays.

Just because something is secular does not mean it is bad. Just because something has the power to conform us does not mean we can never enjoy it in moderation. For example, if you are prone to alcoholism, then you must absolutely avoid alcohol. If you can enjoy a drink in moderation, you are not condemned. The same truth holds for food, movies, parties, and many of the traditional Halloween practices.

The powers and people behind these things may not have our best interests at heart, but we can still find an appropriate amount of joy in them without allowing their influence to corrupt us. Just because someone's sole motive is to get rich off my money does not mean I am wrong for giving that person my money. It is for this reason that I do not care that my phone watches my online activity and listens to what I say to generate advertisements accordingly. I tell my wife all the time that it is not the ad's fault if I am foolish enough to buy something I do not need and cannot afford.

If we are unable to celebrate Halloween because of the consumerism behind the American observance of the holiday, then we probably should not shop at supermarkets either. Regardless of how friendly the folks at your local grocery store might be, someone running the operations is doing so because he or she wants your money.

I respect my separatist friends, those believers who tend to remove themselves from any practices that are not explicitly encouraged in the Bible. My experience with separatism is it becomes very hard to find where to draw the line because our world and our own minds are saturated in sin. No matter how cautious I am in being separate, it is difficult to know for a fact that I am truly avoiding every influence I deem to be potentially corrupting.

I truly believe it is easier to draw the line when you allow yourself to experience those good and enjoyable things in the world when they do not violate a clear teaching of Scripture. An even better approach is to use these aspects of our culture to reinforce spiritual truth, even if biblical teaching was the farthest thing from the mind when that aspect was developed.

(Before I continue, I must clarify that I am writing to a general audience. If there is an aspect of Halloween that makes you uncomfortable because of your own experience and could lead you down a path that will end in sin, then you should avoid what is violating your conscience. It is my responsibility and the responsibility of other believers to encourage you in your approach and not be a stumbling block, even if it means laying down our own rights. For example, again, I would never suggest that it is acceptable for a recovered alcoholic to have a drink, nor would I have a drink in that friend's presence.)

VALIDITY OF REDEEMING CULTURE
Understanding the Difference

As we saw in our survey of Halloween's history, Halloween most likely is already an exercise in cultural redemption. The attendant evidence strongly suggests that the Catholic church moved All Saints Day to November 1 and instituted All Souls Day on November 2 as a response to the Celtic Samhain festival. Rather than abolish pagan practices, the church worked to incorporate into its own culture those practices that could be redeemed.

Perhaps fault may be found in the church's attempt to merge societal practices with religious observance. "Do not be conformed to this world," the Apostle Paul tells us, after all. However, "being conformed to this world" does not mean "participating in culture."

When the New Testament authors use the word "world," often – not always, but often – they are referring to the spirit of this age that is opposed to God. Modern views on abortion, sexuality, and substance abuse are all products of this sense of the term "the world." Carving pumpkins and trick-or-treating are activities that do not carry the same weight on our souls. These activities simply take place in the physical planet we inhabit – the other meaning of "the world," the meaning not intended by Paul in Romans 12.

Yes, we certainly must not shape our faith around our secular society. We establish the foundation of our lives on the truth of God's Word, which supports everything else we build upon it. Participating in sinful practices and allowing ourselves to be indoctrinated by the false teaching of our society is not excusable under the guise of cultural involvement. Skipping church to prepare for an American football viewing party is not permissible just because our culture glorifies sports. This behavior is a clear violation of the fourth commandment, and culture must never conform us to disobey an obvious directive. On the other hand, watching a Halloween movie in which good triumphs over evil cannot as easily be deemed a transgression against God's law.

Remember Jesus said, "I do not ask that you [the Father] take them out of the world, but that you keep them from the evil one," in John 17. I wrote earlier that I find it difficult to draw the line when we tread down the separatist road. Part of this dilemma comes from the truth in Jesus's statement here. It is the Father's will that we remain in this world, which, in this context, is referring to the earth. While our spirits are renewed when we put our faith in Jesus, our bodies remain in this fallen world. Enjoy it for what it is, as long as you steer clear of what is truly evil.

Applying the Difference

When we evaluate a particular cultural practice, it is important to consider what the evidence suggests is the accepted meaning behind it and how it will be taken by the general population. It is not fair for us to impose our own interpretation of something on other people.

Say, for example, I find a circle to be offensive. There is nothing else to this circle. It is just a circle, but I find offense in it for my own personal reasons. I may even have Scripture to defend my position, but the application of that Scripture in this context is unclear. Most people would think my feelings about the symbol are ridiculous. You can feel free to display that symbol in your home without violating your conscience because no evidence or consensus suggests that this symbol is inappropriate, despite my beliefs concerning it.

However, we can all agree that if that circle is replaced with a swastika, it is entirely offensive and inappropriate. It is not just a simple arrangement of lines. There is no redeeming that symbol at this point in our culture because almost everyone knows what it represents, and I imagine that meaning will continue for the duration of time.

Therefore, if the consensus is that carving pumpkins is family fun, you cannot say that this practice is about superstition and expect everyone else to think the same thing. I do not know anyone who carves a pumpkin and sets out a jack-o'-lantern for the purpose of scaring off evil spirits. Even if I did know such a person, most people do not share that motivation.

Similarly, my kids do not knock on a door and say, "Trick-or-treat!" because they are actually going to vandalize that house if they do not get candy. The reason I let them keep the candy is not that I support the greedy desires of confection companies. I do not put out candles in the fall with the hope that they will assist my dead loved ones in their escape from purgatory. It is unfair of us to cast unfounded blame on other individuals who are acting in good conscience for the sake of a harmless experience that is not clearly forbidden in God's Word.

However, we can conclude that there are elements of Halloween, whether in its present or its past, that are clearly inappropriate for believers. The Bible forbids fortune-telling, sorcery, communicating with the dead, and anything else associated with witchcraft (Deuteronomy 18), so pursuing encounters with evil spirits is out of the question. The Bible is clear about humanity's eternal destiny immediately following death, as well as the complete and atoning work of Christ on the cross for our sins; therefore, praying for the dead is pointless. Also, we do not need the Bible to teach us (though it does) that playing pranks that cause physical or emotional damage ought not to be done. Redeeming cultural practices does not mean embracing everything associated with those practices.

You will notice that none of my examples in the previous paragraph included some of the darkest themes of Halloween, namely, fear, evil, darkness, and death. I have heard and read that it is wrong for believers to celebrate Halloween because these themes are unfitting for Christians. Throughout history, Halloween and the holidays that inspired it were inarguably characterized by an obsession with death.

Some people suggest it is wrong for Christians to celebrate Halloween because the holiday cannot be separated from these associations. Personally, I suggest we ask a different question. Rather than ask if Halloween can, in fact, be separated from this celebration of death, I would ask if it even needs to be.

I would confidently answer no. In fact, Halloween's ties with death – and even darkness, fear, and evil – coupled with its mid-fall timing are what make the day such a unique holiday for Christians to celebrate. Here is where we begin to mine the true riches hidden within Halloween.

CHAPTER FIVE

Celebration of Death

Death was not part of the original creation. God is the author of life (Acts 3), and everything he created was good and pure (Genesis 1). Sin brought death into the world, and so we are right in believing death to be a negative aspect of existence. From the fear and discomfort that comes from thinking about or experiencing death, we avoid it and protect our loved ones from it at all costs.

Because of everything wrong with death, we tend to shy away from the topic altogether and, often appropriately, shun anything that has any association with death. Since all through its history Halloween has been tied closely to death and the fear of the unknown that death brings, many well-meaning Christians understandably disassociate with this holiday and question why any believer would dress up or let his or her children collect candy on October 31.

I believe these conclusions against Halloween sprout from a Christian's incomplete view of death. While it is indisputable that death did not exist at the beginning of time and that it is not part of the Christian's ultimate future, death was always part of God's plan. In fact, death is a critical part of God's plan. I might go as far as to say that all of God's plan, from eternity past to eternity future, hinged on death, and you might be hard-pressed to argue against that statement if you continue reading.

WHAT DEATH MEANS FOR JESUS

Jesus Christ is "the founder and perfecter of our faith" (Hebrews 12), and he is the Creator of all things (Colossians 1 and John 1). If we want to establish a correct and complete picture of death, there is no better source from whom to draw than our Lord himself. In addition, we know from the Bible that our Savior is well-acquainted with death and is the only being to ever bring himself out of death, so I consider it only logical to suggest that we begin with Jesus when seeking an accurate understanding of this topic. If we first study what death means for Jesus, we can better understand what death means for those of us who trust him.

"Christ died for our sins in accordance with the Scriptures, . . . was buried, . . . [and] was raised on the third day in accordance with the Scriptures" (1 Corinthians 15). Have you ever stopped to think about why Jesus did it? I do not mean just contemplating the taglines we learned in church. I mean taking time to really think about why the sovereign ruler decided he would die for us.

He died for our sins so we would not have to, yes. The payment had to be death, and it had to be by bloodshed because "without the shedding of blood there is no forgiveness of sin" (Hebrews 9).

To take our place for this kind of punishment truly demonstrates the love of Jesus for us.

The preceding paragraph probably did not teach many of you anything. Those facts are ones you most likely already know. But really think about some of those statements.

Did Jesus die because of some law in the universe stating that sin requires a payment of bloodshed? Was God left with no choice but to exact payment from someone – be it his creation or his Son – because of an immutable law of existence or because of a trick by some evil being or wicked force? Who established this law that sin requires death?

God did! God is the one who says sin requires death. No one forced his hand. He could have made the rules of the universe anything he wanted them to be as long as he was consistent with his character. So why does God require death? Could there not be another way?

Jesus himself gave us the reason: "Greater love has no one than this, that someone lay down his life for his friends" (John 15). Even being the source of all creation and the maker of all the universe's laws, what greater price could Jesus pay than his own life? How better could love be displayed than to give up everything one has, including life itself? Since God is love (1 John 4) and his love extends to the heavens (Psalm 36) – i.e., is limitless – then for God to demonstrate his great love, the highest price imaginable is required. Certainly, the blood of his Son is the highest price that could ever be paid in all existence.

Because of God's eagerness to express to us not just the fact that he loves us but to show us to what unimaginable extent he loves us, death was required. Death was always a part of God's plan. Death is an enemy (1 Corinthians 15), certainly, and is not a personal part of the Christian's ultimate future; however, death is not an outside power with which God was forced to contend. Rather, death is and always was a critical part of God's design.

To Jesus, death means an unmistakable display of the depths of his love for his people. Death is yet another enemy that stands no chance against the sovereign God. Though death is dark and scary, even as it was for Jesus in the moments leading up to his crucifixion (Luke 22), it is nothing that could derail his plan. Rather, it was the very means by which he accomplished his plan. In fact, Jesus rebuked the Apostle Peter for Peter's incorrect response to death (Matthew 16). For Jesus, death was not something to be shunned or avoided.

WHAT DEATH MEANS FOR BELIEVERS

Even though Jesus experienced death for us and conquered it, we must still expect to die. We are not exempt from physical death even after we put our trust in Jesus. This reality is because death still plays an important role for everyone, even Christians.

God, being absolutely sovereign over his whole creation, could have selected a different means for his people to experience his grace. He chose death to be a required part of that experience (with some exceptions, namely Enoch, Elijah, and Christians who are alive at Christ's return). Why God not only allows but ordains painful episodes in our lives is a topic for a whole other book entirely. For now, let us simply trust that God utilizes death in our existence as a necessary means to show us his love and grace.

If the death of Jesus was always part of God's plan – and Revelation 13 does say that the names of those whom Jesus would die for were written down before the world began – then sin was always going to be a required part of existence as well. Jesus was not going to die for nothing because a meaningless death does not demonstrate love.

Even after we put our faith in Christ, we remain under the effects of sin to a very significant extent, both externally in the world around us and internally in our own minds. Although we have been set free from sin through Jesus, we still long to be set free entirely. That freedom, save for a select few people that I mentioned earlier, does not come without death. Even Enoch and Elijah, who ascended to heaven without dying, long to be resurrected.

Romans 6 tells us, "The wages of sin is death." It cannot be debated that death is the payment and punishment for sin. I would like to debate, however, that the topic is a little more complicated than one simple statement.

Death is the unavoidable result of sin, a truth for both believers and unbelievers alike. Even in my 30s, I am well aware that my body is slowing down, wearing out, and dying. Since I have put my faith in Jesus, is this reality my punishment for my sin or is it only a lasting consequence of my sin? If Jesus has borne all my punishment, I would argue my current state is no longer a punishment but simply an irreversible result. Death remains a punishment for unbelievers; it is not clearly so for believers.

Therefore, Christians no longer need to view death, as unpleasant as it may remain, in such a negative light. While death will continue to haunt the wicked, the righteous can welcome it as freedom from the sin that continues to haunt us in this life. In fact, almost as soon as sin entered God's creation, God did not protect the first two people from death, but instead mercifully ensured that they would die. He made certain not that they would continue to live, but rather that they would surely experience death.

In Genesis 3, after the fall of man, the chapter closes out with two acts of mercy on God's part. The first one we usually do not miss is where God "made for Adam and for his wife Eve garments of skin and clothed them." Symbolically, the Lord provides and applies the atonement to cover his children's shame – and, by the way, it came at the cost of something's lifeblood, since those skins did not just appear out of nowhere.

The second act of God's mercy comes in the following verses, where God says,

> "'Behold, the man has become like one of us in knowing good and evil. Now, lest he reach out his hand and take also of the tree of life and eat, and live forever –'" therefore the LORD God sent him out from the garden of Eden . . . . [God] placed the cherubs and a flaming sword that turned every way to guard the way to the tree of life."

I wonder how many people read those verses and see man's banishment from the Garden of Eden and the guarding of the tree of life as acts of God's love. Those actions could easily be misinterpreted as punishments. Here is one of the hundreds of opportunities in the Bible where it helps to think about why the character (in this case, God) is doing what he is doing or saying what he is saying.

God's plan has always been for all of his created people to live forever, whether with him on the new earth or separated from him in the lake of fire. In this passage, God's objective is not to withhold eternal life. His objective is to limit biological longevity.

If Adam and Eve were to eat from the tree of life in their new fallen state, they would continue to live in their sin-cursed bodies forever. There would be no death to set them free from their current condition, and there would be no subsequent resurrection to new life when the King returns. God's plan for us requires death, and so the tree of life needed to be removed from the picture temporarily. The tree of life will make a comeback on the new earth only when sin is no longer a threat (Revelation 22).

Paul said in 1 Corinthians 15, "If in Christ we have hope in this life only, we are of all people most to be pitied. But in fact Christ has been raised from the dead, the firstfruits of those who have fallen asleep." Without an eternal perspective, our hope as Christians in this life is pretty bleak. We can look forward to years, maybe decades, or more of struggling with sin and suffering through difficulty and tragedy until our bodies decompose in the dirt.

Our hope is not in what lies before death but in what lies after death. Why are many of us afraid of the end of this life? Why are we nervous to celebrate a holiday that reminds us of our mortality when with that mortality comes the fullness of our confident expectations?

Halloween gives us an ideal opportunity to reflect on what death means for us as believers. While we do not need to pray for the dead, since no amount of our prayers will ever change a dead person's eternal destiny, it is good to remember the dead and to be aware of death. There is a benefit for us if we honor our faithful loved ones who have gone on before us and share with them the hope of life beyond the grave. For believers, death means freedom from sin and hope of new life, not something to be shunned or ultimately avoided.

WHAT DEATH MEANS FOR UNBELIEVERS

Death, painful and dark though it is, precedes a pleasant ending for Christians. It is not so for the unbelievers, and it is in this context that death is irredeemably hopeless and terrifying. This type of death has inspired the fear and discomfort surrounding the subject. The Christian's hesitancy to celebrate Halloween comes, in part, from the holiday being overtaken by unredeemed people who have a hopeless view of a subject they find frightful.

There is no need to dwell on this topic, as it is indeed sobering to those people who understand its gravity. One who dies in his or her sins remains in his or her sins beyond death. That sin requires separation from God, the source of all good things. This separation begins in hell and ends in the lake of fire (Revelation 20). Even the wicked are resurrected, but only to suffer under God's wrath in their new bodies, bodies which we know very little about but can only imagine are not an improvement over the frail ones we possess now.

For unbelievers, death means hopeless separation – separation from God, other people, and life. As eternity progresses, this separation from all good things will surely make these people only more evil. What is worse, these people would rather be subjected to this dark separation than choose to submit to Christ's rule. Either way, for unbelievers, death is absolutely something to be shunned and avoided.

CONCLUSION

Similar to Christmas and Easter, Halloween is veiled in much tradition, paganism, and commercialization but holds within it a kernel of truth that is worthy of the Christian's attention and celebration. Halloween's connection with death does not invalidate the celebration of the holiday for God's people. If anything, Christians, of all people, should be celebrating it. It is almost ironic that the unrighteous people, the ones who have every reason to fear death, are the ones that confidently engage in Halloween celebrations while many saints avoid the holiday altogether.

As Christians, we have no reason to view death and even suffering as purely negative experiences. It is death that brings about our greatest hope, which is the resurrection of our bodies to live with God forever. Death, although it is our enemy, is the gateway to that blessed hope. The greatest fear of the wicked is a cause of great hope for the righteous.

Even when our faith becomes sight, death will always have a presence in the new world. Isaiah 66 tells us that in the eternal state we "shall go out and look on the dead bodies of the men who have rebelled against me. For their worm shall not die, their fire shall not be quenched and they shall be an abhorrence to all flesh." It is clear from this passage and what we know from other portions of Scripture that the writer is not referring to bodies that are biologically dead.

First of all, as I stated before, God created all people to live forever, one way or another. Second, the mention of "fire" is a clear reference to the lake of fire we read about in Revelation 20. Isaiah is envisioning the rebels who are spiritually dead but very much alive biologically. These are the damned.

On the new earth, we, who are free from the effects of sin and death, will be able to put eyes on those people who are dead in the worst way possible, forever cursed to bear the weight of their own sin. This death is an ongoing yet static state, never to be altered. Its presence remains into eternity as an endless torment for unbelievers and a humbling reminder for believers that God is great in love and mercy toward those children whom he has delivered.

A disclaimer is necessary at this point. While death is a necessary part of God's plan for everyone, including Christians, it is also critical that we remain in these bodies until God decides it is time for us to go. The hope of a better fate on the other side of the grave is not an incentive for us to become careless with our lives or suicidal. Such behavior would be plummeting to the other side of the spectrum. We do not need to fear death; however, we must remain cautious against it.

The Apostle Paul seemed to have struck the ideal balance in this regard when he wrote in Philippians 1,

"For to me, to live is Christ and to die is gain. If I live in the flesh, that means fruitful labor for me. Yet which I shall choose I cannot tell. I am hard pressed between the two. My desire is to depart and be with Christ, for this is far better. But to remain in the flesh is more necessary on your account."

As great as our destiny is beyond this life, we are responsible to fulfill our mission here as long as we are breathing.

The conclusion of the matter is that death is not to be avoided at all costs, nor can it be. As Christians, we can redeem the world's obsession with it and celebrate the hope we have even when faced with death. Halloween is not a day of which Christians should be afraid. Halloween is an opportunity for believers to be distinctly different, to look at reality through the lens of Scripture, and do things in a better, more meaningful way than the world could ever be capable of doing.

CHAPTER SIX

Return of Christ

Halloween's association with death along with its mid-fall timing point to an event on God's timeline of equal significance to those events celebrated at Easter and Christmas. Christmas looks back on the Messiah's first coming. Easter looks back on the Resurrection of the Messiah. Halloween looks ahead to the Messiah's return.

Death carries hope for a believer because the believer looks forward to being resurrected when Jesus Christ returns. Incidentally, the Bible suggests that Jesus will return during the time of year that is immediately followed by Halloween. This timing makes Halloween all the more appropriate to be used by Christians to celebrate the coming resurrection without altering the history and tradition that has made Halloween what it is today.

I know as soon as I say the Bible points to the fall as the time of year when Jesus returns, most readers will immediately quote Matthew 24 where Jesus said, "But concerning that day and hour, no one knows," or Luke 12, which states, "You also must be ready, for the Son of Man is coming at an hour you do not expect." Jesus makes very specific statements here, and just because Jesus will return suddenly and without warning, the Scriptures do not preclude the ability to narrow the event down to a particular season. In fact, once we have gone through a couple passages of Scripture, I think you will see there is a very compelling argument to be made that the weeks leading up to Halloween are, in fact, the time of year the King will return.

To make my case, I go to Leviticus 23. I suppose an Old Testament passage would not be the first place most people would turn when studying the Lord's return, especially an excerpt from Leviticus. If you were then to see the topic that is covered in Leviticus 23 before continuing in this book, many of you will likely start to wonder what the Jewish feasts could have to do with the Second Coming. I believe the fall feasts on the Jewish calendar provide a timeline of the Messiah's second coming, and I intend to explain why I hold this belief. To do so, I will address each of these three feasts in chronological order, and, as we go, I will make my case for what each one appears to represent on God's agenda for the end times.

FALL FEASTS
Feast of Trumpets

The first half of Leviticus 23 outlines the spring feasts. We will briefly come back to these feasts later, but since we are focusing on the fall season in this book, the latter half of chapter 23 is what pertains to our topic. The first of the fall feasts mentioned is the

Feast of Trumpets. This feast, along with the other two we will quickly study, is still kept by the Jewish people today; we may just know them by different names.

Today, the Feast of Trumpets is referred to as Rosh Hashanah, which you will likely see on your calendar somewhere in September, right around the start of autumn. "Rosh Hashanah" means "head of the year" and serves as modern Israel's new year festivity, right around the same time the ancient Celtics held their new year celebration of Samhain. At the time of the institution of the Feast of Trumpets, however, the feast did not signal the start of the first month of the year but rather the seventh month on the Hebrew calendar (Tishrei today; formerly called Ethanim).

Leviticus 23 gives just a little bit of information on this feast, but I think it is enough to point us to a couple other passages in Scripture to draw our conclusions. I encourage you to study the history and current keeping of these feasts on your own, as there is always more insight to gain from biblical truths when we consider the historical context. However, to be succinct, that depth of study is not necessary for this book.

Verse 24 is all we need right now: "In the seventh month, on the first day of the month, you shall observe a day of solemn rest, a memorial proclaimed with blasts of trumpets, a holy convocation." I know on its own, that verse does not present a lot of useful information. At best, you may make the connection between the trumpet blasts in this verse and the blast of the last trumpet at Christ's second coming mentioned in 1 Corinthians 15. You may suggest it is a tenuous connection, and I would agree with you if that much information were all the evidence we had. By itself, that conclusion is quite a reach.

However, it is helpful to note what trumpets were used for in ancient Israel, and we find that information in Numbers 10. Two silver trumpets were made, and they were used "for summoning the congregation and breaking camp." Later in the chapter, we read of another use: "When you go to war . . . then you shall sound an alarm with the trumpets, that you may be remembered before the LORD your God, and you shall be saved from your enemies."

Trumpets were used in ancient Israel to call the people together, to prepare for war, and to be remembered by God for salvation from their enemies. Let us go back to 1 Corinthians 15 now, where Paul tells us that the resurrection of the dead and the rapture of those believers who are alive at that time are preceded by the sounding of the trumpet. Earlier in the chapter, we read that the resurrection and rapture occur "at [Christ's] coming," so we can conclude that the trumpet signals Christ's return. We get a picture of Jesus's return in Revelation 19, where the Apostle John writes,

> *"Then I saw heaven opened, and behold, a white horse! The one sitting on it is called Faithful and True, and in righteousness he judges and makes war . . . . And the armies of heaven, arrayed in fine linen, white and pure, were following him on white horses. From his mouth comes a sharp sword with which to strike down the nations, and he will rule them with a rod of iron. He will tread the winepress of the fury of the wrath of God the Almighty."*

Amen! Even so, come, Lord Jesus! The beginning of Revelation 20 gives information on the resurrection, explaining that

> *"the souls of those who had been beheaded for the testimony of Jesus and for the Word of God, and those who had not worshiped the beast [the Antichrist] or its image and had not received the mark on their foreheads or their hands . . . came to life and reigned with Christ for a thousand years. The rest of the dead did not come to life until the thousand years were ended. This is the first resurrection."*

There is one detail about the end times that does not seem to come up in this passage or at all throughout Revelation. It happens to be a topic over which we often obsess: the rapture. Paul mentions the rapture in 1 Corinthians 15 when writing about the blast of the last trumpet when he says, "We shall not all sleep, but we all shall be changed, in a moment, in the twinkling of an eye, at the last trumpet." He also speaks of it in 1 Thessalonians 4, which says,

> *"For the Lord himself will descend from heaven with a cry of command, with the voice of an archangel, and with the sound of the trumpet of God. And the dead in Christ will rise first. Then we who are alive, who are left, will be caught up together with them in the clouds to meet the Lord in the air, and so we will always be with the Lord."*

From these verses, we know that the rapture and the first resurrection occur simultaneously at Christ's return. However, John appears to leave the rapture of surviving believers out of his prophecy for some reason.

I argue John did include all the raptured saints in Revelation 19, where it says, "And the armies of heaven, arrayed in fine linen, white and pure, were following him on white horses." I suspect the "armies of heaven" are the raptured and resurrected believers who form Christ's army. Of course, the armies of heaven could simply refer to angels, as is more commonly assumed. However, I have a couple reasons to believe people like you and I comprise this army.

Staying in that same verse, the soldiers are described as wearing "fine linen, white and pure." John uses this type of language elsewhere in Revelation:

- "Yet you have still a few people in Sardis, people who have not soiled their garments, and they will walk with me in white, for they are worthy. The one who conquers will be clothed thus in white garments, and I will never blot his name out of the book of life" in Revelation 3;

- "Buy from me . . . white garments so that you may clothe yourself and the shame of your nakedness" also in Revelation 3;

- "Then they were each given a white robe and told to rest a little longer, until the number of their fellow servants and their brothers should be complete," in Revelation 6;

- "A great multitude . . . standing before the throne and before the Lamb, clothed in white robes" in Revelation 7;

- "These are the ones coming out of the great tribulation. They have washed their robes and made them white in the blood of the Lamb," also in Revelation 7;

- "'His bride has made herself ready; it was granted to her to clothe herself with fine linen, bright and pure' – for the fine linen is the righteous deeds of the saints" earlier in Revelation 19.

One of John's themes in Revelation is fine white linen, and it almost always refers to people who have been redeemed and have carried out God's will. I would be remiss to leave out that Revelation 15 describes "the seven angels with the seven plagues" as "clothed in pure, bright linen." It does not use the word "white," as in most of the other passages I listed, but one could still argue that this white attire is not exclusively associated with humans. However, the odds are stacked in Revelation that the white linen of the armies of heaven may be hinting that the meeting of believers that Paul details in 1 Thessalonians 4 is not some party in the sky but a gathering for war – signaled by the sound of the trumpet, just as the instrument was used in ancient Israel. If this theory is true, then get ready to strap on your sword.

Besides, 1 Thessalonians 4 ends with, "So we will always be with the Lord." If we meet Jesus in the air on his way down, then we are coming back with him. The only other beings I see who are with Jesus in Revelation 19's picture are the armies of heaven. The Messiah's conquest is detailed in the remainder of Revelation 19, and it can be assumed that Jesus's army is very much involved in this battle.

Just like the trumpet was used in ancient Israel to gather the people, to prepare for war, and to be remembered by God to bring about deliverance, so it seems that the last trumpet will gather God's people, prepare them for war, and keep them in God's memory following the Great Tribulation. It is not only the use of trumpets, though, that leads me to believe that Rosh Hashanah signifies the day Jesus will return, but also the time of the month that the feast commences.

Leviticus 23 tells us that the Feast of Trumpets is held on the first day of the month during the fall season. The Hebrews kept track of months by the cycle of the moon: one cycle of the moon equals one month. It was the new moon that signaled the start of a new month, and so the seventh moon of the year also brought with it the Feast of Trumpets.

The timing of this feast might be a key to indicating its future fulfillment. The problem with seeing a new moon and thus anticipating the moment Jesus will potentially return is that this stage of the lunar cycle is when the moon's illuminated side is facing away from earth. It is virtually impossible to see a new moon from the earth's surface because it blends in with the sky. Because of this phenomenon, it could be said that "concerning the day or the hour, no one knows" when the new moon begins. Where have we heard those words before?

The evidence suggests that the Feast of Trumpets looks ahead to a time when Israel's Messiah will declare war on Israel's enemies, an event that never occurred during Christ's first time on the earth. With the revelation of New Testament truth at our disposal, we now know that this event coincides with the return of Jesus. This particular holiday typically comes several weeks before Halloween, but both are still considered fall holidays, and Halloween's theme of hope after death certainly draws a connection with Christ's return.

Day of Atonement

If Rosh Hashanah is the holiday that points to Christ's return, it might make more sense to celebrate the September holiday itself rather than wait until October 31. I think that decision would be getting ahead of ourselves, though, since the Feast of Trumpets only begins the fall festivities for the Jewish people. As we continue in Leviticus 23, we read of another holy day just nine days later: the Day of Atonement, or Yom Kippur, as it is said in Hebrew and is better known today.

God describes the Day of Atonement in Leviticus, saying,

> *"Now on the tenth day of this seventh month is the Day of Atonement. It shall be for you a time of holy convocation, and you shall afflict yourselves and present a food offering to the Lord. And you shall not do any work on that very day, for it is a day of atonement, to make atonement for you before the Lord your God."*

This day was the one day of the year when the high priest entered the Most Holy Place of the Tabernacle or Temple to offer sacrifices for his own sins and for the people of Israel. Its significance to the ancient Israelites is obvious for that reason, yet it likely points to another event that has yet to occur. I believe we find Yom Kippur's fulfillment in Revelation 20, shortly after the fulfillment of Rosh Hashanah.

In Revelation 20, John writes,

> *"Then I saw an angel coming down from heaven, holding in his hand the key to the bottomless pit and a great chain. And he seized the dragon, that ancient serpent, who is the devil and Satan, and bound him for a thousand years, and he threw him into the pit, and shut it and sealed it over him, so that he might not deceive the nations any longer, until the thousand years were ended . . . . Then I saw thrones, and seated on them were those to whom the authority to judge was committed."*

In John's vision, there is no sacrifice for sin. There is no bloodshed. There is no priest. It is fair to question how this picture could be analogous to the Day of Atonement celebrated by Israel. My answer is that there are two sides to our atonement. On one hand, we need to be cleansed from our own sinfulness. Personal sin is why the high priest entered the Most Holy Place year after year.

However, when Jesus died, the curtain to the Most Holy Place was torn (Matthew 27), and our sins were paid for in full. There is no need for the priest to continue to offer sacrifices on Yom Kippur, as those sacrifices could never take away sin anyway (Hebrews 10). This part of our atonement is complete because Jesus accomplished it during his first coming.

While our personal sin has been washed away, we still long for atonement from the sin in our world that continues to haunt us. We no longer need to be cleansed. We need the world to be judged. It is this event that I believe is foreshadowed by the Day of Atonement, a day during the fall when, perhaps nine days after his return and after subduing his enemies, the Lord will take his place not as Priest as he did at his first coming, but as Judge.

In the first portion of Revelation 20, we see first that Satan is judged, fulfilling Christ's statement recorded in John 16 ("the ruler of this world is judged"). Then we read that, after years, decades, maybe centuries of waiting, we receive our vindication from the evil of this world. Since the point of this book is to defend the celebration of Halloween, a full exposition on eschatology is not necessary; however, what is necessary for this portion is that, at the very least, humanity and Christians in particular will have come out of a very trying time before the return of Jesus. Once the Messiah has subdued his enemies, he will establish his judgment and finally vindicate his glorified followers of all the evil they have endured for the past seven years and prior.

Feast of Booths

The Day of Atonement pushes our celebration of Christ's return out another week or so. There is still one more feast in Leviticus 23 that the Jews celebrate in the fall and, like the Day of Atonement, reminds us of a time in the past while looking ahead to a time in Israel's future. This celebration is called the Feast of Booths or, as it is called nowadays, Sukkot (which means "booths").

Continuing in our passage, the Word of God says,

> *"Speak to the people of Israel, saying, 'On the fifteenth day of this seventh month and for seven days is the Feast of Booths to the Lord . . . . When you have gathered in the produce of the land, you shall celebrate the feast of the Lord seven days. On the first day shall be a solemn rest, and on the eighth day shall be a solemn rest . . . . You shall dwell in booths for seven days. All native Israelites shall dwell in booths, that your generations may know that I made the people of Israel dwell in booths when I brought them out of the land of Egypt.'"*

It is helpful to remember that the term "booth" here could also be translated as "tent" or "tabernacle." Those terms might bring to mind the Tabernacle that the Israelites erected at each of their stops during their wilderness wanderings. Among other things, the Feast of Booths reminds the Hebrews of the time when God dwelt with his people. Might I suggest that it also brought to their minds a time in the future when God would dwell with his people again?

I cannot speak for every Jew, but I suspect that the Apostle Peter, at least, saw a connection between the Feast of Booths and the Messiah's Kingdom. In Matthew 17, we read of Christ's Transfiguration, to which Peter was a witness. Matthew writes,

> *"Jesus took with him Peter and James, and John his brother, and led them up a high mountain by themselves. And he was transfigured before them, and his face shone like the sun, and his clothes became white as light. And behold, there appeared to them Moses and Elijah, talking with him. And Peter said to Jesus, 'Lord, it is good that we are here. If you wish, I will make three tents here, one for you and one for Moses and one for Elijah.'"*

In my personal experience, the consensus is that Peter was muttering nonsense in this passage because he was overwhelmed with what was occurring and had been rendered nearly speechless. I do not believe that explanation to be the case. It seems more likely to me that Peter's Jewish mind was making a connection with Scripture – as Jewish people often do.

You see, while I can come up with a television or movie quote at least once a day to fit my current situation, the Jews, the guardians of God's law, were thus saturated with the Scriptures. It is not a stretch at all to think that the Jewish mind, confronted with the

Messiah in his glory on a mountain, would conjure the prophecy found in Zechariah 14. This passage reads,

> *"Behold, a day is coming for the Lord, when the spoil taken from you will be divided in your midst. For I will gather all the nations against Jerusalem to battle . . . . Then the Lord will go out and fight against those nations as when he fights on a day of battle. On that day his feet shall stand on the Mount of Olives . . . . Then the Lord my God will come, and all the holy ones with him . . . . And the Lord will be King over all the earth. On that day the Lord will be one and his name one . . . . Then everyone who survives of all the nations that have come against Jerusalem shall go up year after year to worship the King, the Lord of hosts, and to keep the Feast of Booths."*

Peter was a man well-versed in the Scriptures. He lived among a group of people who were constantly reminded of different portions of what we refer to as the Old Testament. Peter was already convinced that Jesus was the Messiah, and was eager to see the Kingdom established. As soon as the Messiah started shining like the sun on a mountain alongside two departed saints, I think it is not a stretch at all to think Peter's mind went to Zechariah's prophecy that the Messiah would stand on a mountain, defeat his enemies, and establish his Kingdom.

Since the prophecy continues on to say that the Feast of Booths will be kept when the Kingdom is established, Peter's exclamation about setting up tents makes more sense. Perhaps Peter, clearly mistaken though he was, was not uttering quite as randomly as readers often assume. There are portions of this Old Testament passage that were clearly not being fulfilled during the Transfiguration, such as the mountain's splitting or all the saints' joining Jesus, but there are enough details here to suspect what Peter was thinking.

While, as with any of these feasts, it is unclear how exactly Sukkot will be fulfilled, the significance of this feast at the return of Jesus may be tied to the event with which it is already clearly associated: the wilderness wanderings. While Israel was in the wilderness, God dwelt with them in the Tabernacle.

When Jesus sets up the Kingdom, God will again dwell with man. This time, however, since the curtain has been torn, the King will walk among his people, no longer confined to a structure. I imagine that the Feast of Booths, which according to this timeline would begin two weeks after Christ's return, will be the official establishment of the Millennium, the inauguration of King Jesus.

First Kings 8 may also give us a hint as to the meaning behind Sukkot. We read in this passage that at the completion of the Temple under Solomon, a feast that lasted eight days was held in the seventh month of Israel's calendar. While the text does not specifically refer to this feast as the Feast of Booths, the Feast of Booths is the only regular eight-day feast during the seventh month. Possibly this celebration was a separate, one-time feast initiated by Solomon for the dedication of the Temple as well; the connection, however, is undeniable.

During the festivities, Solomon blessed the people of Israel and dedicated the Temple. It was in this Temple that God would dwell among his people and issue blessings to them if they remained faithful to him, just as he did from the Tabernacle in the wilderness. Given the timing and nature of the event recorded in 1 Kings 8, we have here possibly a foreshadowing of the blessing and dedication to come at a Sukkot celebration in the future.

In fact, just as Leviticus 23 has walked us through the fall feasts in chronological order, it runs parallel with the events that are predicted in Revelation 19 and 20. We have already studied the return of Jesus and the following judgment. Next in Revelation 20, we read, "And I saw the souls of those who had been beheaded for the testimony of Jesus and for the Word of God . . . . They came to life and reigned with Christ for a thousand years."

After Jesus defeats his enemies and vindicates his people, he sets up his Kingdom alongside his saints, presumably right at the time that the Feast of Booths is celebrated. It is probably not a coincidence that all of these events take place at harvest time, which is when Sukkot begins. Once Jesus has reaped his spiritual harvest, the Millennium will commence.

Literal Timing

Perhaps you see the connection between the fall feasts of Leviticus 23 and the events predicted in Revelation 19 and 20 enough to be convinced, like I am, that the chapters are connected. Maybe, however, you think I am reaching when I suggest that the timing of the Lord's return and the events following will be fulfilled as specifically as the days given for the feasts. You might be wondering if I am taking a questionable leap to even suggest that Jesus will return in the fall. After all, just because the feasts that point to the Messiah's return take place in the fall, it does not mean they have to be fulfilled in the fall too, and certainly not fulfilled in such rapid succession. While one could make the case that the timing of the feasts could be unrelated to the timing of their fulfillment and do so without contradicting Scripture, I believe the Bible gives a convincing precedent that strongly hints that the fall feasts will be fulfilled in the feasts' literal timing. I hold this belief because it has happened before.

Remember that the fall feasts are preceded in Leviticus 23 by the spring feasts. The spring feasts inarguably point to events that occurred at Christ's first coming, and it stands to reason that the fall feasts will be fulfilled at Jesus's second coming in much the same way the spring feasts were fulfilled.

Since an in-depth study of the spring feasts is unnecessary for an argument in favor of Christians' observance of Halloween, I will not spend nearly as much time here. My only point is to show how literally the spring feasts were fulfilled. What we find here will help us know what to expect concerning how the fall feasts will be fulfilled.

Leviticus 23 lists three spring feasts: the Passover coupled with the Feast of Unleavened Bread, the Feast of Firstfruits, and the Feast of Weeks. Allow me for each to briefly detail the information pertinent to our current study. Note how literally every one is fulfilled.

- The Feast of Unleavened Bread was to be kept on the fifteenth day of the first month on the Jewish calendar (Nisan), the day after the Passover, which looked back on the time when Israel was preparing for the Exodus. God slayed all the firstborn sons of the Egyptians, passing over the Israelite dwellings when he saw the blood of a lamb on the doorposts. Immediately following, the Jews escaped their bondage in Egypt. This feast was fulfilled when Jesus's blood was shed on the cross so that the Father would pass over us in judgment, allowing us to escape from our bondage in sin. Jesus's crucifixion took place immediately after the Passover feast.

- The Feast of Firstfruits occurred in the spring when the Israelites would begin to grow the new year's crops. Their first harvest would be given to the priest on the day after the Sabbath. Since the Sabbath was (and remains) a Saturday for Jews, the day after the Sabbath would be our Sunday – the very same day of the week that Jesus rose from the dead as a "firstfruits of those who have fallen asleep" (1 Corinthians 15). This feast was kept the Sunday after the Passover, and the Resurrection occurred the Sunday after Jesus was murdered.

- For the Feast of Weeks (or Harvest), the Israelites would present a multitude of sacrifices to the priest. It was to be held 50 days after the Feast of Firstfruits ("the day after the seventh Sabbath," so this feast was also on a Sunday). Not coincidentally, we read in Acts 2 that the Holy Spirit birthed the church at Pentecost exactly 50 days after the Resurrection.

I have to admit before I did my own study on all the feasts in Leviticus 23, I already believed Jesus was coming back in the fall but had my own concerns that maybe I was grasping a little at some of the other conclusions. However, after seeing how the spring feasts were fulfilled at Christ's first coming – to the very day! – I am convinced not only that Jesus will return in autumn to fulfill the fall feasts but that the order of events will coincide perfectly with the timing of these feasts. Given the specific fulfillment of these spring feasts and God's penchant to keep his Word literally as it is, it would contradict logic to think the events of Revelation 19 and 20 will not fulfill the feasts of the latter half of Leviticus 23 in like fashion. I would be awfully surprised if they did not. My faith would not be shaken though, since God does have a way of surprising us.

Current Observance

Bringing this teaching back to our point that Christians can and should celebrate Halloween if done so in good conscience, when we consider the fall feasts as a whole, we move from the start of fall to a date several weeks later in the season. The end of Sukkot could be as late as October 25 – less than a week before Halloween, making Halloween the ideal time of year to celebrate the culmination of Christ's return and the first resurrection. In light of a Christian Halloween's theme of hope after death – specifically, the hope of resurrection after Christ's return – I would argue it is not at all a reach to redeem Halloween to celebrate in advance the King's return, judgment, and reign to counteract the curse of death. In that case, we can put Halloween right up there with Easter and Christmas when it comes to Christian significance

PART III
CAUSE
—FOR—
CELEBRATION

CHAPTER SEVEN

Reasons to Celebrate

There is a lot more to Halloween for a Christian than ghosts, candy, and costumes. By themselves, there is nothing scripturally forbidden about these aspects of the mid-fall holiday, and wholesome fun should be encouraged among believers, not condemned. However, if it is spiritual truth for which you are looking, Halloween is loaded with it as well.

Even if Halloween is to be regarded as a celebration of death, there is nothing wrong with that viewpoint from the Christian perspective. It is important to be reminded of our mortality, as it encourages us to make the most of the time we have, to honor the people who have gone on before us, and to dwell on the hope we have as believers in Jesus. When boiled down to its core, Halloween for the Christian is about the hope of resurrection upon the Lord's return.

RESPONSE TO OPPOSITION

I am not suggesting that every Christian should be compelled to celebrate Halloween. Observance of this holiday is a matter of conscience. It is certainly not a requirement, just like we are not obligated to participate in Christmas or Easter festivities. In fact, I suspect the fundamental reason any of us celebrates the birth or resurrection of Jesus at specific times during the year has more to do with our culture than our faith. We put out a jack o'lantern for the same reason we put up a Christmas tree: it is what our friends and families did when we were growing up. If our society did not celebrate these holidays, we probably would not either, at least not to the extent that we do.

Halloween has a questionable reputation among believers because of all the dark themes associated with it. I hope our study of the holiday's history and the biblical truths associated with it helped clear up some of the smoke that has obscured the redeemable truth behind Halloween. In fact, some of the evils that have come to be associated with Halloween have nothing to do with it.

For example, in our survey of the initial inspirations and historical celebrations of Halloween, we saw no mention of Satanism. Some people have confused Halloween as being associated with the devil because of the ancient belief of demons crossing over to our world during Samhain or Stingy Jack's bargain with Satan. The truth is, however, there is no reason to believe that Satanic rituals heighten during the Halloween season or that anyone who celebrates Halloween is any more likely to be a worshiper of Satan.

Murder is another topic that has become falsely tied to Halloween. Serial killers have no place in the history of this holiday. Personally, I hardly consider movies about murderers to have a place among our culture's Halloween favorites. I am not saying all movies about killers are irredeemable and inappropriate for believers; I am simply saying those kinds of movies do not strike me as Halloween movies for the fact that murderers are irrelevant to the history and truth behind the holiday. All that blood and gore was introduced to Halloween by Hollywood to make money. It is not fair to disown Halloween because of the misuse of the holiday by other people or corporations.

While witchcraft is a prominent theme during Halloween, it came to be through fear of those individuals who were thought to be dabbling in the dark arts. This time of year did not bring with it an invitation to participate in communing with the dead or committing sorcery. The wrongful practices of sinful people during the Halloween season are not a reason for us to throw out the good with the bad.

Just because we are called to be separate does not mean outsiders need to think we are weird. We do not have to wear clothes that are different from unbelievers as long as we are dressed modestly. We do not have to watch different movies than unbelievers do as long as those movies contain redemptive qualities. In the same spirit, it is acceptable to celebrate holidays with pagan origins or that were influenced by false teaching as long as we do not embrace those false beliefs as part of our observance. Better than simply enjoying these aspects of our culture, we can redeem them to remind ourselves of and point others to the truths of the Bible.

MOTIVATION TO REDEEM

As I have gained experience, especially as a father, I have found that if you are reasonably creative and biblically trained, it is not hard to find Christian themes all around us in our secular culture. It fascinates me how even unbelievers are unknowingly attracted to the themes of the Gospel to the point where it shows up subtly in their own works, more proof of God's image within all of us. Many of our movies, books, television shows, and holidays present opportunities for us to engage with our culture and connect it to Christ. These are opportunities that we miss if we insist on separating ourselves from everything that does not explicitly mention Jesus.

There are actually many good, biblical causes for celebration at Halloween. For the Jews and the Celtics, to name just two people groups, this time of year was a time to celebrate the harvest and be thankful for having their needs met. Halloween is a good opportunity to thank God for his continued provision and protection as we go into the cold winter months. For me, though, this reason takes a backseat, since Thanksgiving Day is a holiday that already matches these criteria.

Remember that in 1517 the Reformation began on Halloween night. Today, many reformed Protestants replace Halloween with Reformation Day, and it is a good thing to celebrate the reformers who paved the way for us to have a complete and personal understanding of the Scriptures. Naturally, such a celebration may alienate some of your Catholic friends, and the Reformation has little to do with Halloween other than sharing the same date on the calendar, thanks to Martin Luther's response to the false teaching surrounding Allhallowstide. Still, it is never an inappropriate time to celebrate truth.

Most prominently, we can celebrate death. Yes, celebrate it. Not because of its devastation. Not because it is to be taken lightly. Celebrate it because it sets us free. Celebrate it because it is our release from what holds us down in this life. Celebrate it because it is a necessary step toward our great hope of resurrection when Christ finally establishes his long-awaited Kingdom.

I know death is a topic we have already dealt with at length. To be honest, when I first began to participate in Halloween festivities as an adult, I drew the line here. I did not need ghosts or gravestones in or near my house because I thought death was associated with the enemy, and I wanted to be clear that we celebrate life in my house.

However, it became harder and harder to hold this line, not because I wanted to include cute ghosts and harmless zombies with my celebration, but because, in all sincerity, as my conviction grew for why Christians should not just ignore Halloween but actually earnestly embrace it, I realized this celebration has everything to do with death and that it is good to celebrate death. In John 12, Jesus himself said, "If it dies, it bears much fruit."

Celebrate those faithful loved ones who are now with Jesus. Wait with them for the blessed hope of the appearance of our Lord. Weep because we no longer get to enjoy their company for a time but rejoice because their pain is over.

Celebrate Halloween because Halloween pictures our freedom in Christ. I have no problem participating in festivities that are saturated in reminders of evil, fear, and darkness. To the Christian,

Halloween itself is a reminder that we are no longer enslaved to these elements, and they have everything to do with the hope we recognize at this time of year.

- Evil cannot touch us if we are kept by the Lord. However, we also cannot ignore evil either, as its presence remains very real in this world. What an opportunity Halloween presents us to remind ourselves and teach our children about the reality of evil and its eventual eradication!

- Fear is banished by God's love. We have been delivered from fear and are no longer crippled by it, like so many people in the world are. The more we rest in God, the more foreign fear becomes to us. At Halloween, we can celebrate our freedom from fear rather than revel in fear's false power.

- Darkness is our opportunity to be light in its midst. The light shines brightest in darkness. We cannot shine God's light if we hunker down in our houses to wait out what has been falsely termed "the devil's holiday." People need to see the light.

Look forward to the return of Jesus, just like the Israelites did, perhaps unknowingly, during their fall feasts. We already celebrate the other major events of Christ's life (namely, his birth and the Resurrection). If we truly believe his return is only a matter of time and not a matter of his trustworthiness, then we might as well begin celebrating. After all, God already considers us "glorified" (Romans

8). Jesus's return is so certain that he's as good as here already, so break out the apple cider and have a pumpkin spice donut.

Of course, you do not need a religious reason to celebrate Halloween. Harmless fun is just that – harmless. You can have a Halloween party without putting Bible verses up. You can enjoy a tastefully scary movie without looking for biblical themes. You can take your kids trick-or-treating without having Jesus on your mind. Would it not be better, though, if you did add a spiritual component to your festivities? Why pass over an opportunity to further renew your mind and teach your children?

At the very least, you and your family get harmless fun out of celebrating Halloween. Incidentally, you will have a lot of opportunities to be involved in your community. Whether you are handing out candy or taking your kids to a community fall event, Christians need to be involved in the world around us to maximize our potential to share the good news of Jesus.

Appropriately involving oneself in culture works only to give credibility to our witness for Christ, not hinder it. All of those benefits can come just from a fairly passive involvement in Halloween, which is an opportunity largely unlike other holidays that are typically spent with people we already know. While you are at it, if you can actively find ways to take what the world has corrupted and turn it into spiritual lessons for yourself and your family, then everyone is even better off for it.

CHAPTER EIGHT

Ways to Celebrate

In this final chapter, I want to take everything we have studied throughout this book and give you some ideas for how to practically celebrate Halloween. Along with my suggestions, there will be some cautions because this book would not exist if not for the discomfort among Christians surrounding this holiday. I will repeat again that whether or however you choose to celebrate Halloween, "be fully convinced in [your] own mind," as Paul tells us in Romans 14. In the same chapter, Paul tells us, "Whoever doubts is condemned . . . . For whatever does not proceed from faith is sin."

If your conscience is trained by the Bible, then embrace the celebration of Halloween. Have fun with it! Use it as a tool to train up your children on the themes associated with Halloween. Just, again, be sensitive to a brother or sister who may question what you do or who may find offense in it. Respect his or her decision to abstain from your celebration. On the other hand, if you have made it this far in the book and you maintain that Halloween is not a holiday that will be recognized in your house, refrain from condemning your brother or sister who does celebrate the holiday out of a pure conscience.

MEANS OF CELEBRATION
Replacing Halloween

In the previous chapter, I already began to refer to some possible festivities that would be appropriate for the days leading up to and including October 31. Since the ancient Jewish and Celtic festivals celebrated the harvest, we would not be the first people to take Halloween as an opportunity to do the same.

Many Christian churches have "harvest parties" in place of Halloween celebrations, where children get to play games, hear the gospel of Jesus, and still get to dress up and go home with a ton of candy. It is deemed safer than going door-to-door, has a strong Christian emphasis, is an opportunity for outreach in the community, and the kids still have a lot of fun. For Christian parents who are wary of Halloween, a church harvest party is a good alternative.

I personally do not prefer this option for a few reasons. A harvest party misses the opportunity to celebrate the rich truths behind Halloween that we have studied in this book and fails to replace them with anything unique. I mentioned previously that Thanksgiving Day is already a time set aside to thank God for his provision in our lives, so using a harvest theme in place of Halloween, to me, is redundant. I suspect most church harvest parties have more to do with letting kids celebrate Halloween without calling it Halloween than it does with celebrating the harvest season.

Also, while I am in favor of the idea of the church reaching out to its community, pulling all the parents who go to that church into the same location on Halloween prevents those parents from being a testimony in their individual neighborhoods. I would argue that the church is more about sending people out than it is about pulling them in. I wonder if a trick-or-treat stop at the church with a few volunteers would be a good compromise.

Finally, as long as you take your kids to a safe neighborhood that you trust, there really is not an equally fun replacement for going door-to-door and yelling "trick-or-treat!" when you are a kid. A harvest party does not provide children with this once-a-year activity. Of course, your children may actually end up with more candy at a harvest party, but does it really matter, from a parent's perspective, how much sugar they get?

Another Halloween replacement idea that I mentioned earlier is a Reformation party in honor of Martin Luther's posting of his 95 Theses on October 31, 1517. Much like a harvest party, your kids can play games, get candy, and dress up – as their favorite reformer. Personally, as of the time of this writing, I doubt either of my kids even knows of a single reformer, let alone has a favorite one. My main question is that if I decide to attend a Reformation party dressed up as John Calvin, how will people know I am Calvin without telling them?

Believe me, I love the reformers and the Reformation. I have already mentioned that I am a reformed Christian myself. In fact, there are not many Christians my age who are prouder to be reformed. Even I think a Reformation party risks coming off as cheesy. Let us certainly celebrate the Reformation at this time of year. Let us listen to sermons and have Bible studies about salvation by grace alone through faith and the authority of Scripture. Let us just also dress up as ghosts and watch Halloween movies too. Besides, I would be very surprised if a Reformation party garnered much attention from the unbelievers in the surrounding community.

Embracing Halloween

I recognize that I was a little hard on the replacement parties. Sincerely I say go for the replacements if it is where your conscience guides you. My point is that we can be distinct without being considered weird. Obviously, I am pro-Halloween and I embrace the truths and the fun that come with this holiday. My suggestions for observing Halloween are not going to be very different from what typical tasteful Halloween celebrations already look like. The differences are the intentionality behind each choice and the confidence of knowing where to draw the line.

Decorations

The best place to start is to decorate. I like to live in the moment and embrace whatever the current season is. For me, decorations enhance the joy of each season. The stereotype is that women are generally the ones who are excited to decorate and that men typically do not care or notice. I do not fit that stereotype. I do the decorating in my house because I love doing it. By mid-September, I have already pulled out the Halloween decorations in my basement just so that they are ready to go as soon as it is time to put them up.

I try to be intentional with what I put up for Halloween, and I encourage you to do the same. For example, I do not have a problem with putting up ghosts because people recognize ghosts as the spirits of the dead. As Christians, we know that when a brother or sister in Christ dies, his or her spirit is free with the Lord – a truth we celebrate at Halloween. Those smiling little apparitions in white burial shrouds hanging around my house are reminders to me of the truth of eternal life after death even before we return to the earth in our resurrected bodies.

Speaking of resurrected bodies, I am in favor of zombies too. I did not used to be, but then I thought about Daniel 12, which says, "Many of those who sleep in the dust of the earth shall awake, some to everlasting life, and some to shame and everlasting contempt." That verse is about as purely a Halloween Bible verse as you are going to find. We all recognize zombies as the "undead," or, more simply, resurrected bodies of people who have died.

Even their typically grotesque appearance is appropriate among Halloween's themes: these essentially less-than-humans rising from their graves are a reminder that the wicked who refuse to trust and obey our King will rise at the end of the Millennium as something far less than the human condition with which we are acquainted today. Decaying zombies can serve as a humbling reminder of what is at stake in this life. Conversely, the righteous will rise again fully human, a better and truer version of humanity than what we are now.

Monsters, too, can be depicted well within the bounds of what is appropriate for Christians at Halloween. We consider monsters to be unnatural beasts who inspire terror. Monsters can be used as a training tool for our children to reveal the true nature of sin. Dress sin up on the outside any way you want, but underneath it is still monstrous and unnatural for redeemed humanity.

Another idea is to remind your children that monsters are not real and cannot cause harm, so there is no need to be afraid. Remember that, for believers, Halloween is not a celebration of fear but rather a celebration of freedom from fear. When my daughter sees a scary monster at Halloween time, I use it as an opportunity to tell her that this is the time of year that we celebrate the fact that we do not need to be afraid because Jesus takes care of us. The difference here is that the fears we have been freed from are still very real; they have simply lost their power over us.

Some of the most appropriate decorations for Halloween are skeletons and gravestones. I mentioned before that I used to push associations with death outside the bounds of what Christians incorporate into their Halloween festivities. Now that I have a more complete understanding of what death means to believers, I embrace the use of skeletons and gravestones because they are very much Christian themes that fit right in with the celebration of this holiday.

If you are trying to think of a Bible passage that mentions skeletons, many of you may already have brought to mind Ezekiel 37 where God brings the dry bones back to life. In the same chapter, he says, "I will open your graves and raise you from your graves." For Christians, graves and skeletons are not symbolic of a scary and hopeless fate. They are reminders of a temporary state that precedes our hope of rising again.

So put the skeleton in your porch chair on Halloween night. Put gravestones in your front yard, maybe homemade ones with Bible references to the resurrection and the eventual defeat of death and evil. I admonish you not to run away from what the world has used for bad when you have an opportunity to redeem it for good. Skeletons and graves have everything to do with what Christians should celebrate at Halloween.

The typical orange and black color scheme of Halloween is significant too. Orange is associated with the harvest season since many of the changing leaves and much of the food that is gathered at this time of year are this color or close to it. Black, as you likely already know, is connected to death. Whether it is Samhain, All Saints, or Halloween that is being celebrated, all of these holidays acknowledge the significance of death during this time of year, be it death in nature or of loved ones. For these reasons, the colors orange and black have been used in celebrations of this point in the year since ancient times. We have established that both harvest (orange) and death (black) are important topics in Scripture, so go ahead and deck your house in these colors.

Activities

Besides decorating, there are a slew of activities you and your family can do at Halloween. A simple online search will give you countless craft ideas, and plenty that incorporate Bible verses and themes. If you lead or participate in a Bible study, use this time of year to study the resurrection, death, fear, evil, or even the Jewish fall feasts. (After all, it was a Bible study that inspired this book.)

Similar to Halloween decorations, you can do many of the usual things you already do at Halloween, only with more intentionality. Watch a tasteful Halloween movie or television show, so long as good triumphs over evil. Point out what redemptive themes you can identify in it. Carve a jack o'lantern with your kids and roast the seeds as a fun, seasonal snack. Tell your children that just like you did with the pumpkin, God picks us out, cleans out the junk, and puts a light in our hearts and a smile on our faces. Get out in the community and go to pumpkin farms, trunk-or-treats, and family-friendly haunted houses. Come up with your own inspirations behind your activities as you allow your conscience to be guided by the Holy Spirit!

Then comes the big night when it is perfectly acceptable for Christians to participate in trick-or-treating. Dress in whatever tasteful costumes you want, and if you can put together a Christian theme with it, even better. The first time my family went trick-or-treating together after coming to the realization of the spiritual truths behind this holiday, my daughter wanted to be Elsa from Frozen, so my wife and I dressed up as a king and queen and used the theme of royalty as a reference to when the resurrected saints will reign with Christ. Use the creativity God gave you, and feel free to use any of the creatures from the section about decorations and anything in addition to those that you want to consider in good conscience.

Have a Halloween party. Consider opening it up to your neighborhood rather than just inviting people you already know. After all, the incredible opportunity we have at this time of year is reaching out to the people around us, people who need to see the light of Jesus amidst dark times. I am not suggesting you preach a sermon at your party or hand out gospel tracts instead of candy (if you do give out tracts, give the kids candy too). A friendly invitation and a cheerful demeanor can go a long way to creating more opportunities for witnessing in the future without the risk of coming off to your neighbors as simply odd.

If you host a party or give out candy on Halloween, the children in your community are literally walking up to your door! It is the one day of the year when minimal effort gives you a chance to testify to the grace in your life. Why are we avoiding this opportunity? Even if you are uncomfortable with Halloween, buy some candy and kindly greet the children who knock on your door. You do not have to put up decorations or take your own kids out (in that case, I would suggest buying enough candy to have some leftover treats for your children).

Halloween is actually one of the biggest days of the year in my family at my own home. Most other holidays are hosted at other relatives' houses, but Halloween belongs to the Sargeants. Every year we decorate our garage with cobwebs, bats, spiders, and ghosts (all fake, of course) and develop crafts and games for the neighbors to enjoy. We have lights strung from the rafters and a fog machine operating while LED candles and strobe lights flicker. On the television is a slideshow of Bible verses related to the themes of Halloween while recognizable Halloween music plays. In addition to handing out candy, we put out cider and donuts to make our house as welcoming as possible for the big night. It is a hit every year. Even if no one gets saved in our garage, our standing in our neighborhood is established, and the opportunity for Christian witness is enhanced, not hindered.

I suppose you could do the same thing and cut the scary stuff out if you wanted. You would be in harvest party territory at this point, and I would wonder if everyone would grasp how your chosen theme has anything to do with Halloween. The outreach element is still there, though, and I would think it a neat stop for my own children during the night regardless. Still, my suggestion is, given the unique nature of Halloween, to embrace the holiday for all the good that is in it.

CAUTIONS AGAINST CELEBRATION

As much as I recommend celebrating Halloween, I feel strongly about not doing so until you have fleshed out your own understanding of the background and Scriptural truth behind it. Given the mass misunderstanding of this holiday among believers, it is very easy to violate your own conscience or a brother or sister's conscience if you do not proceed with caution. My prayer is that this book will suffice in your personal endeavor, but I am not conceited enough to suggest that you would not be benefited from seeking other sources to enhance your knowledge on these subjects.

Because of the controversy over this holiday among Christians, I think it is wise to put thought and meaning behind your celebration. Be intentional with your activities, decorations, and even your costumes. Then again, I have already said that I believe it is not a sin to celebrate Halloween just for fun, even without religious motivations. You can dress up as Batman just like you can attend a sporting event for the lone purpose of being entertained. My only concern with celebrating Halloween in a purely secular manner is that you are missing a great opportunity for Christian witness and could be unnecessarily confusing some of your friends who may be more conservative than you.

I went into some detail in this chapter already about ideas for redeeming concepts of Halloween that you, your friends, and your family can enjoy. The list was not exhaustive, and just because I did not make mention of something does not mean that I find it inappropriate. As I said before, feel free to apply your own creativity to the many facets of Halloween's celebration. However, there are a few elements that I did not include in the previous portion of this chapter because I personally do exercise caution when considering them, and I would suggest you do the same.

High Alert

First of all, while Halloween does not have satanic roots, modern Halloween is rife with associations with Satan and demons. Demons and hell are depicted in various means of Halloween celebrations, including movies, decorations, and costumes. There are well-meaning Christians who include these elements in their festivities and say that the use of satanic elements is a means of taunting the devil since we are no longer under his power and thus have no reason to fear him. That explanation does fit well under my thoughts about the use of fearful themes, so I do not hold judgment against believers who embrace this type of practice.

I am personally uncomfortable with it, though, because it brings unnecessary attention to satanic spirits and, in a way, glorifies them since I doubt Satan's feelings are hurt when he is taunted. He is our enemy, and we are warned in 1 Peter 5 to "be sober-minded [and] watchful. [Our] adversary the devil prowls around like a roaring lion, seeking someone to devour." Demons are not, in my opinion, a redeemable evil, and we do not want to treat irredeemable evil flippantly.

This stance does not necessarily exclude movies or television shows with demonic characters. For example, murderers are evil beings too, yet most of us do not have qualms about watching a movie that includes someone being maliciously killed. The killer is an antagonist, and the redeemable value of his or her presence in the film is determined by the character's outcome – does he or she repent from or face justice for his or her crimes, or are those crimes glorified? Repentance and justice are biblical themes; the exaltation of wicked behavior is inconsistent with ultimate reality and not redeemable for Christians. In like manner, a demonic character may be treated as any other villain in a show or movie.

Halloween's rise to prominence in America had much to do with Hollywood's treatment of the subject of killing. The movie industry shamelessly added gore, violence, and murder to this season, where these subjects were unrelated to the holiday before the 20th century. Gore and violence for the sake of shock value are, in my humble opinion, unnecessary and too casual for redeemed believers. Blood is precious to God, and it should be to us.

I am not saying violence needs to be excluded entirely from our entertainment. Such an approach would require us to be excessively separate, as these realities exist in our world. However, we and our children need no more than to be aware of their presence in our current existence. Knowing the extent to which these evils can go is not required for us to be sober-minded regarding the subject. Besides, these themes have nothing to do with the history and background of Halloween, so their inclusion is pointless, especially in a Christian celebration of the holiday.

Speaking of themes that have nothing to do with Halloween's background, decadence and sensuality have no place in a Christian holiday celebration. This type of behavior is irrelevant to an earnest observance of Halloween and is clearly unbecoming of a Christian. Using the cultural celebration of Halloween as an excuse to drink excessively, do drugs, and wear unnecessarily revealing costumes is not an example of redeeming culture.

Wearing a costume for your spouse privately is your business. What you do publicly, however, impacts the people around you, and you are accountable for those actions. Alcoholism and drug abuse are sins, as is lewd behavior. These elements need to be excluded and avoided by Christians when it comes to Halloween celebrations.

Cautious Wisdom

There are a couple elements often associated with Halloween that I believe are a little trickier to decipher. I will not come down as strongly against them as I did in the previous section of this chapter, mainly since my personal stance on them is still unresolved to some extent. However, caution is necessary, and the wisdom of Scripture must guide your conscience as you make your own determinations as to whether or not these elements have any place in your personal celebration of Halloween.

Some haunted houses appear to go beyond what is appropriate for a Christian's celebration of Halloween. I think the cute, modest one in your garage or down the street at your neighbor's house is all in good fun and should not be discouraged. These types of haunted houses can be good outreach opportunities if utilized correctly, and there is no harm as long as the shock value is low. Anything that is generally deemed appropriate for children is most likely all in good fun, and this holiday is meant to be fun more than anything else.

However, especially frightening haunted houses, like the ones you have to pay for to get in, are designed to shock the participants and glorify fear for the sake of fear. While getting scared a little bit can provide its own thrill to an appropriate extent, I wonder if these haunted houses that inspire fear for fear's sake are missing the point if included in a believer's celebration of Halloween.

Then there are the "Christian" haunted houses, better known as hell houses, that attempt to scare the participants by showing shocking images of the results of sinful living. Perhaps the right motivation is behind the project, but the execution is questionable at best. Jesus did not commission us to shock or scare people into loving him. Besides, it is difficult to shock anyone these days with what we can see in a movie or at a high-budgeted commercial haunted house, so a non-profit church would have to work pretty hard – likely too hard – to try to do so.

Instead of trying to scare people, just share Jesus with them. The love of Christ is not scary. In fact, "perfect love casts out fear" (1 John 4). If the secular haunted house is missing the point of redeemed Halloween, then a Christian hell house is most certainly missing that point.

The last topic I want to cover is witchcraft. The Bible is clear that witchcraft is forbidden for believers (Deuteronomy 18). While Scripture excludes the practice of sorcery and divination as part of our practice, it could be argued that it is still all right to include witches in our Halloween decorations and costumes. I fear the use of witches may belong under the same category as demons since both are real and rebellious. Witches used as characters in movies and television shows would be handled similarly then, where the portrayal and outcome of the character determine its redeemable use in a story.

However, witches in particular often fall into the category of fantasy, not horror, where there are witches and wizards on either side of good and evil. It is essentially an alternate reality created for fun and entertainment. A good example of this type of world is the Harry Potter series – a series full of Christian themes and redeemable elements.

I must admit while my family generally avoids incorporating witches into our Halloween celebration, we also enjoy the occasional viewing of the Harry Potter movies. It is a complex issue, so I respect the opinions of people whose own dealing with this topic lands them on either side of the fence – or on the fence itself, which I suppose is the case with me.

I know this chapter was not exhaustive, and it was not intended to be. My intention was to give several examples of what could be redeemable and what probably is not redeemable so that you the reader have an idea of how to put thought into your own decisions regarding the celebration of Halloween and come to conclusions that will allow you to act in good conscience, regardless of your stance about this holiday.

It is my prayer, as we reach the conclusion of this book, that the history of Halloween that we have studied along with the Scriptural truths associated with the prominent themes of this holiday will allow you to form a basis on which you can develop your own celebration of this often-misunderstood festivity. May what you decide bring encouragement to your own souls and those of your family, friends, and community, as well as bring glory to our coming King, whom we wait for and celebrate at this and any time of the year.

Epilogue

Incorporating the historical church's use of Halloween and the truths of the Bible that connect this holiday to our faith, my family has developed several reasons for which to celebrate on October 31 and the days leading up to it. We hope for the return of our Lord and Savior Jesus Christ. We await our resurrection from the dead. We remember those faithful loved ones who died before us, who, too, will rise with us after Jesus returns. We revel in our victory over evil, fear, and death. Most of all, we celebrate to be the light in the darkness, the light that the world needs to see. There is no better day to be the light than on the holiday that the world considers to be the darkest.

I hope this book has helped clear up the misconceptions surrounding Halloween as well as clarify the redemptive quality of the questionable elements that remain. Since Christians are called to be light in the darkness, separating ourselves from everything that initially causes us to question its appropriateness would be a disservice to the people around us who need our encouragement and outreach, including our own children. There are plenty of things about Halloween that can be redeemed, especially when we understand the truth behind its celebration, even if many of those facets still are not inherently spiritual in nature.

As with other elements in our culture, including holidays like Easter and Christmas that we not only celebrate but consider the highest holy days of the Christian year, we can redeem Halloween for Christian use. I highly recommend it because not only will your family and friends have fun with it, but you will also have a truly unique opportunity to be light in darkness without sacrificing the acceptable secular enjoyment that comes with many of Halloween's themes and traditions.

One more time I will admonish, though, to be guided by your conscience, and be sure that your conscience is guided by the Bible as you are led by the Holy Spirit. To violate your conscience or to disregard the concerns of a brother or sister in Christ is a sin. Halloween, probably more than any other holiday celebration, has the potential to unnecessarily offend, so do be cautious. I hope that some of my remarks have helped in that regard, for both those of you who are determined to celebrate Halloween earnestly and those of you who still think it best to avoid or replace the holiday. You have my respect either way.

Maybe those ideal fall days I mentioned at the start of this book are what the first days of the Millennium will feel like. Perhaps the next time you hear the crisp leaves crunch under your shoe, you will, like I, grow excited in anticipation of the Savior's return someday, most likely around this time of year. Just as those leaves change and fall, so too will the current age. Dwell on the hope that you have of new life in Jesus and on your current freedom from sin, evil, darkness, and death, though we must continue to experience measured amounts of it for some time still. There is much to celebrate and much to be excited for from the very start of the fall season, culminating in the festivity originally monikered All Hallow's Eve.

Surely there is sorrow that comes with this celebration as well. With tears, even as I type, I think of my friend Ron, my mother-in-law I never met, and my three precious babies that never saw light in this world. But I wipe my tears away because it does not have to be sad, and it is certainly not scary. There is hope. That hope is bright, and that hope is why my family celebrates a holiday associated with death. That hope, when the rest of the world sees only evil, fear, and darkness, is what makes us light in that darkness. We celebrate Halloween because people need to see that light.

HALLOWEEN BIBLE VERSES
Evil

"Even though I walk through the valley of the shadow of death, I will fear no evil, for you are with me." *Psalm 23:4*

"The face of the LORD is against those who do evil, to cut off the memory of them from the earth." *Psalm 34:16*

"The LORD will keep you from all evil; he will keep your life." *Psalm 121:7*

"Do not be overcome by evil, but overcome evil with good." *Romans 12:21*

"The Lord will rescue me from every evil deed and bring me safely into his heavenly kingdom." *2 Timothy 4:18*

Fear

"The LORD is my light and my salvation; whom shall I fear? The LORD is the stronghold of my life; of whom shall I be afraid?" *Psalm 27:1*

"I sought the LORD, and he answered me, and delivered me from all my fears." *Psalm 34:4*

"When I am afraid, I put my trust in you." *Psalm 56:3*

"God gave us a spirit not of fear but of power and love and self-control." *2 Timothy 1:7*

"There is no fear in love, but perfect love casts out fear." *1 John 4:18*

Darkness

"Arise, shine, for your light has come, and the glory of the LORD has risen upon you. For behold, darkness shall cover the earth, and thick darkness the peoples; but the LORD will arise upon you, and his glory will be seen upon you." *Isaiah 60:1-2*

"You are the light of the world . . . . Let your light shine." *Matthew 5:14 & 16*

"To give light to those who sit in darkness and in the shadow of death." *Luke 1:79*

"I am the light of the world. Whoever follows me will not walk in darkness but will have the light of life." *John 8:12*

"Be blameless and innocent, children of God without blemish in the midst of a crooked and twisted generation, among whom you shine as lights in the world." *Philippians 2:15*

Death

"Precious in the sight of the LORD is the death of his saints." *Psalm 116:15*

"The memory of the righteous is a blessing, but the name of the wicked will rot." *Proverbs 10:7*

"He will swallow up death forever; and the LORD GOD will wipe away tears from all faces." *Isaiah 25:8*

"The last enemy to be destroyed is death . . . . Death is swallowed up in victory. O death, where is your victory? O death, where is your sting?" *1 Corinthians 15:26 & 54-55*

"[I am] the Living One, I died, and behold I am alive forevermore, and I have the keys of Death and Hades." *Revelation 1:18*

Resurrection

"Your dead shall live; their bodies shall rise. You who dwell in the dust, awake and sing for joy! For your dew is a dew of light, and the earth will give birth to the dead." *Isaiah 26:19*

"And many of those who sleep in the dust of the earth shall awake, some to everlasting life, and some to shame and everlasting contempt." *Daniel 12:2*

"And you shall know that I am the Lord, when I open your graves, and raise you from your graves, O my people." *Ezekiel 37:13*

"An hour is coming when all who are in the tombs will hear his voice and come out, those who have done good to the resurrection of life, and those who have done evil to the resurrection of judgment." *John 5:28-29*

"For since we believe that Jesus died and rose again, even so, through Jesus, God will bring with him those who have fallen asleep." *1 Thessalonians 4:14*

Christ's Return

"The trumpet will sound, and the dead will be raised imperishable, and we shall be changed."
1 Corinthians 15:52

"Our citizenship is in heaven, and from it we await a Savior, the Lord Jesus Christ, who will transform our lowly body to be like his glorious body." *Philippians 3:20-21*

"The Lord himself will descend from heaven . . . . And the dead in Christ will rise first." *1 Thessalonians 4:16*

"Then I saw heaven opened, and behold, a white horse! The one sitting on it is called Faithful and True, and in righteousness he judges and makes war. His eyes are like a flame of fire, and on his head are many diadems, and he has a name written that no one knows but himself. He is clothed in a robe dipped in blood, and the name by which he is called is the Word of God. And the armies of heaven, arrayed in fine linen, white and pure, were following him on white horses. From his mouth comes a sharp sword with which to strike down the nations, and he will rule them with a rod of iron. He will tread the winepress of the fury of the wrath of God the Almighty. On his robe and on his thigh he has a name written, King of kings and Lord of lords." *Revelation 19:11-16*

"Behold, I am coming soon, bringing my recompense with me, to repay each one for what he has done. I am the Alpha and the Omega, the first and the last, the beginning and the end." *Revelation 22:12-13*